Finding My Voice
Kids with Speech Impairment

Kids with Special Needs

Finding My Voice
Kids with Speech Impairment

by Sheila Stewart and Camden Flath

MASON CREST PUBLISHERS INC.
370 Reed Road
Broomall, Pennsylvania 19008
(866)MCP-BOOK (toll free)
www.masoncrest.com

First Printing
9 8 7 6 5 4 3 2 1

ISBN (set) 978-1-4222-1727-6   ISBN (pbk set) 978-1-4222-1918-8

Library of Congress Cataloging-in-Publication Data

Stewart, Sheila, 1975–
  Finding my voice : kids with speech impairment / by Sheila Stewart and Camden Flath.
       p. cm.
  Includes bibliographical references and index.
  ISBN 978-1-4222-1722-1   ISBN (pbk) 978-1-4222-1925-6
  1. Speech disorders in children—Juvenile literature. I. Flath, Camden, 1987– II. Title.
  RJ496.S7S744 2010
  618.92'855—dc22
                              2010010009

Produced by Harding House Publishing Service, Inc.
www.hardinghousepages.com
Design by MK Bassett-Harvey.
Cover design by Torque Advertising Design.
Printed in the USA by Bang Printing.

Photo Credits
Creative Commons Attribution 2.0 Generic: eyeliam: p. 25, WellSpringCS: pg. 41; Creative Commons Attribution Share Alike 2.0 Generic: adobemac: pg 39, ceejayoz: pg. 36, hoyasmeg: pg. 42, pawpaw67: pg. 38; GNU Free Documentation License, Version 1.2: LifeArt: pg. 32; MorgueFile Free License: phaewilk: pg. 35; United States Department of Defense: pg. 31.

The creators of this book have made every effort to provide accurate information, but it should not be used as a substitute for the help and services of trained professionals.

Introduction

To the Teacher

Kids with Special Needs provides a unique forum for demystifying a wide variety of childhood medical and developmental disabilities. Written to captivate an elementary-level audience, the books bring to life the challenges and triumphs experienced by children with common chronic conditions such as hearing loss, intellectual disability, physical differences, and speech difficulties. The topics are addressed frankly through a blend of fiction and fact.

This series is particularly important today as the number of children with special needs is on the rise. Over the last two decades, advances in pediatric medical techniques have allowed children who have chronic illnesses and disabilities to live longer, more functional lives. At the same time, IDEA, a federal law, guarantees their rights to equal educational opportunities. As a result, these children represent an increasingly visible part of North American population in all aspects of daily life. Students are exposed to peers with special needs in their classrooms, through extracurricular activities, and in the community. Often, young people have misperceptions and unanswered questions about a child's disabilities—and more important, his or her abilities. Many times, there is no vehicle for talking about these complex issues in a comfortable manner.

This series will encourage further conversation about these issues. Most important, the series promotes a greater comfort for its readers as they live, play, and study side by side with these children who have medical and developmental differences—kids with special needs.

—*Dr. Carolyn Bridgemohan*
Boston Pediatric Hospital/Harvard Medical School

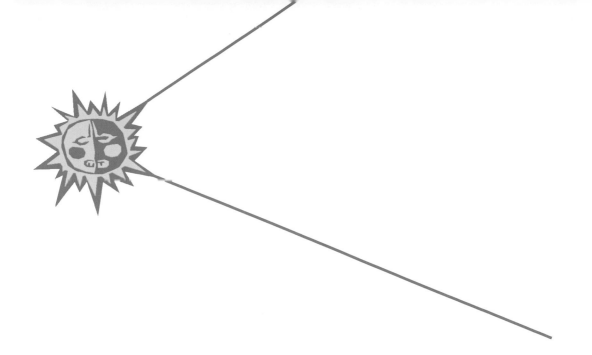

Today was a bad day. A bad, bad day.

Everything started off normal, but then Mrs. Bennett stood up and said, "We're going to be starting a research unit. You will each pick a topic that interests you and read and learn about it. In two weeks, you'll be giving presentations to the rest of the class, to share what you have learned."

I thought I was going to pass out. Seriously. Yeah, I know—fainting guys are just funny, not cool. But just thinking about standing up in front of the class and talking made me dizzy. That's because I can't always talk. I might know what I want to say, but the words don't always want to come out of my mouth. They get stuck and they trip over each other.

I've stuttered for as long as I can remember. When I talk in front of people, I get scared that I'll stutter, and that kind of makes it worse.

So now I just stared at my desk and took deep breaths. I was hoping Mrs. Bennett would say, "Just kidding!" or even, "You can work with a partner and only one of you will have to give the presentation." But she didn't.

I was shooting hoops with my friends Dante and Cara during recess, when Kevin Jones started messing with me.

"Hey, Eric," he yelled, "How are you gonna do that pr-pr-pr-presentation when you st-st-st-stutter so bad?"

"Shut up, Kevin!" Cara yelled, before I could even open my mouth. She's such a girly girl that if you just looked at her you'd never think she'd like basketball or that she could be so loud. I glared at her. I didn't want Kevin to think I couldn't stick up for myself.

I didn't know what to say to Kevin, but I had to say something. So I said, "I'll just do the presentation like everyone else." Except that it didn't come out like that. I stumbled over the word "just" and then I couldn't get the word "presentation" to come out at all. Kevin laughed and ran off with his friends while my face turned red.

"What a jerk," Dante said. He threw me the ball.

"Don't worry about him," Cara added.

But I was worried. I couldn't even get through a sentence without stuttering, so how was I supposed to do a whole presentation? When I stood up in front of the class, Kevin wouldn't be the only person laughing at me.

I threw the ball so hard it bounced off the rim and went flying off across the playground.

At home that night, I was still in a bad mood. We had pizza for supper, and usually that would have made me happy, but not tonight. Mike and Chris, my big brothers, were laughing and talking about basketball practice. They're nice guys, I guess, but they're perfect, and that bugs me. They're both on the basketball team, and they both get good grades. Mike plays the piano and Chris plays the saxophone. They're good looking and popular. And neither of them stutters.

I'm nothing like them. I'm not horrible in school, but not great. Not horrible in sports, but not great. I used to take piano lessons, but I was so bad that Mom and Dad finally let me quit. I'm normal looking and I have a few friends, but I'm not popular. I don't think I'm really good at anything. I'd just be a normal, average kid if it weren't for the stuttering thing.

"What about you, Eric?" Dad asked suddenly, when Mike stopped talking long enough to take another bite of pizza. "How was school today?"

"O-okay," I said. "N-nothing special."

Mom looked at me, trying to decide whether something was wrong. I don't usually stutter that much at home.

So I smiled innocently and took a big bite of pizza. I didn't want to talk about it.

After supper, I went to my room. I turned on some music and pulled out my homework. It was hard to think about math, though, because that stupid presentation was the only thing on my mind.

There was a knock, and Mom stuck her head in the door.

"I know there's something wrong," she said, "so you might as well tell me now."

For about a second, I tried to decide whether or not I should tell her, but then I just blurted it out: "I have to do a presentation in front of the class."

"What's the presentation about?" Mom sat down on my bed next to me.

"What does that matter? Nobody's going to l-listen to anything I have to say anyway. They'll just be l-l-laughing at me because I st-st-stutter."

Mom looked like she was going to get mad, but all she did was mutter, "Kids are so mean." Then she hugged me.

"There will always be some nasty people," she said. "Ignore them as well as you can and just do your best. If you care about what you're saying, people will listen."

Maybe, I thought, but I still have to be able to say it.

The next day in school I had speech therapy in Mr. Spencer's office. Twice a week, I went to see the speech therapist in his office, and once a week he came to class to see me. I liked Mr. Spencer, but I knew what he was going to say when I told him about the presentation.

"Yeah, that sounds scary," he said. "But I know you can do it. Have you been using your tools?"

And that's what I knew he would say. I'm not very good at the tools, though. Mr. Spencer said I needed to keep practicing. Part of the problem is that I should have started working on them a long time ago, but my

family used to live in the middle of nowhere, and my speech therapist there was nice but she didn't know very much.

"Right," I said. "The tools."

We both looked at the poster on his wall. On the top it said "Eric" and below that it said,

- Relax your speech muscles (especially your vocal folds and your tongue).
- Easy Talking—ease into your words.
- Stretchy Speech—stretch out your vowel sounds just a little.
- Don't try to speak too quickly.

"What do you think you want to do your presentation about?" Mr. Spencer asked.

I sighed. There was that question again.

"Why don't you do it on stuttering?"

Later that day, Mrs. Bennett gave us time in the library to start researching our presentation topics, but I still didn't know what my topic should be. I didn't really like Mr. Spencer's idea about doing a presentation on stuttering. Stuttering was something I didn't want to think about at all if I could help it. Dante was going to do his on firefighters, and Cara was going to do hers on Venus and Serena Williams. I tried to think of everything I liked.

Umm, football, basketball, superheroes . . . I started thinking about how nobody would listen to anything I had to say because of the stutter. I thought about Mr. Spencer's idea again. Maybe it wasn't such a bad idea. Then, if I stuttered, I could just say it was part of the presentation.

I found a couple of books about stuttering on the shelves and took them back to the table. How was I going to do this?

"Hey, that's a good idea," Cara said, looking at the books.

"Maybe." The thought of the presentation was still making me want to be sick.

"Just ignore Kevin," Dante said.

He always knew what I was thinking.

Two weeks later, the night before the presentation, I was in my room trying to practice. I had made a slide show on the computer and I'd written out everything I wanted to say, but I was just as nervous as when Mrs. Bennett had first told us we had to do a presentation. More, probably, since now I had to give the presentation in something like fourteen hours.

"Knock, knock," Dad said, opening my door. "How's it going?"

"Not great."

"Do you want to practice on me?" Dad asked.

"No." I was sick of this whole thing, to tell the truth. I just wanted it to be over. If I was going to do it, I wanted it to be great, but I didn't know if I could do that.

"Okay," said Dad. "Now, when you give the presentation tomorrow, remember to look people in the eyes.

And if you get nervous, they say to picture people in their underwear."

"What? I can't talk to a bunch of people in their underwear! I'd just get distracted!"

"Hmm," Dad said. "Well, think of everyone as a good friend who really wants to hear what you have to say. And don't think about Kevin!" he added.

Even my dad knew about my Kevin problems.

The next day I couldn't eat at all. All morning, I was shaking, deep down in the middle of me.

The presentations had been split up over a few days and there were two people ahead of me today. First, a girl gave a presentation about her cat. She was nervous and kept forgetting what she was going to say. Even though it felt mean, that cheered me up a little. The next presentation was by a guy who was talking about how a car engine worked. He seemed to really like engines, but I couldn't pay attention. Any minute now, it would be my turn. My hands were icy cold.

The kid who'd been talking about engines sat down. This was it. Everyone turned around and looked at me. I stood up slowly and walked to the front of the class.

There are only nineteen kids in my class, but when I looked at them from the front of the room, they looked like hundreds. Dante and Cara were smiling at me, and Mr. Spencer was in the back giving me a thumb's up. I didn't look at Kevin.

I found the slideshow file on Mrs. Bennett's computer and pulled up the first slide so that it was projected on the screen beside me. "What's in a Stutter?" the words on the slide said in big, black letters.

I took a deep breath. "E-e-every superhero has a w-w-weakness," I said. "Sometimes it's k-kryptonite. S-sometimes it's a bad temper. Sometimes it's a st-stutter. Do you know how many amazing people had to overcome stuttering? Bruce Willis stuttered when he was a kid, and now he's a famous actor. The Vice

President, Joe Biden, stuttered when he was a kid, and now l-look where he is."

I kept going. I told them about how nobody really knows exactly what makes people stutter, but that humans are the only creature known to stutter. I told them about all the parts of your body that go into talking, like your vocal folds and your tongue and your brain. I told them about some of the ways people treat stuttering and how some of them work better for some people and others work better for other people, but that all of them take a lot of hard work. I got them all to try stuttering themselves, so they could feel what it was like—sort of.

I was almost done. "I'm not really that interested in stuttering," I said. "It's something I d-deal with every day, but it's not what I want to spend my l-life thinking about. There are lots of things I'm more interested in, and maybe if we have to give another presentation sometime I'll t-t-tell you about those things. You can a-a-ask me about stuttering if there's something you want to know, and as long as you're not being a jerk, I'll t-tell you. Or you can forget the stuttering and treat me like a normal kid, because that's what I am."

At first the class was totally silent when I stopped talking, but then Cara started clapping, and then Dante and everybody else joined in.

"That was great!" Dante said as I sat down.

My legs were really shaky, and I felt a little dizzy. And I felt really, really glad to have finally gotten that presentation over with. It hadn't even been as bad as I'd been afraid, and I hadn't stuttered as much as I had worried about.

Mr. Spencer walked over and put his hand on my shoulder. "Great job, Eric! I'm really proud of you."

I glanced over at Kevin. He wasn't looking at me, just frowning and staring out the window. At that moment, I didn't even care if he hadn't heard a word I said. Like my mom had said, some people were always going to

choose to be nasty, and if he wanted to be one of the nasty ones, that wasn't up to me.

But I knew a lot of people had heard what I'd said. For a lot of my life, I hadn't wanted anyone to hear me talk, but now I realized that I kind of liked being listened to and being heard.

Suddenly, I was determined to work harder at speech therapy. I had a lot of things I wanted to say.

Kids with Speech Impairment

We need speech and language to talk with others about facts, thoughts, and feelings. Every day we share information about what we are thinking, how we are feeling, and what we want and need. Many people, including many young people, however, are unable to use speech in the same way that others do.

> An **impairment** is something that gets in the way of a person being able to do something.

Those with a speech or language *impairment* may have trouble using the parts of the body needed for

Language and speech are important to our world.

speech. They may have problems using language correctly, or they may make one sound when they're trying to say another. A speech impairment might limit the ability of a child or student to say certain words, make some sounds, or speak at all. A language impairment may prevent students from learning, understanding, or using language correctly in school. Speech and language impairments can get in the way of kids doing well in school. They can make life harder for kids outside the classroom too, with their friends and the people they meet.

> *Disabilities are conditions—either mental or physical— that keep a person from being able to do whatever others can.*

Speech and language impairments are challenges to be faced by the kids who have these *disabilities*. These children, however, are usually just as smart and friendly as any other student. They may take longer to learn to use language, have trouble speaking, or difficulty making certain sounds—but they can be good at many other things. They are worth getting to know!

How Does Speech Work?

You may not have ever thought about it—but speech is complicated. Each word you speak uses many different parts of your body working together to produce the sounds that are turned into words.

Speech begins in the brain. After your brain decides it has something to say, you breathe air into your lungs. As you breathe in, two strands of muscle in your throat called vocal folds (or vocal cords) move closer together. When

> **Vibrate** means to move back and forth very quickly. This motion can sometimes make sound.

you breathe out, these vocal folds *vibrate*, making

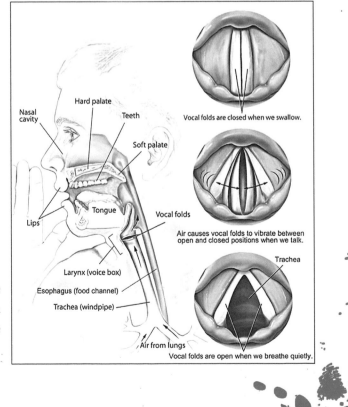

Nasal cavity

Hard palate

Teeth

Soft palate

Lips

Tongue

Vocal folds

Larynx (voice box)

Esophagus (food channel)

Trachea (windpipe)

Air from lungs

Vocal folds are closed when we swallow.

Air causes vocal folds to vibrate between open and closed positions when we talk.

Trachea

Vocal folds are open when we breathe quietly.

This image shows the parts of your mouth and throat that are used when you talk.

27

sound. By changing the amount of air you breathe in and the way you breathe out, you can change the way you are speaking. You use the movement of your lips, tongue, and jaws to make different sounds or words. The size and shape of your nose, mouth, throat, and vocal folds is what makes your voice different from anyone else's.

The process of speaking depends on all of these body parts working together, from the brain to the lips and tongue. With so many steps in the process, many things can go wrong, causing speech impairment. If someone

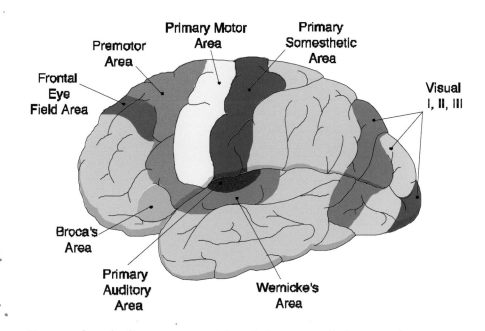

Your vocal cords, lips, tongue and jaws help you speak, but your brain starts everything. Different parts of your brain control different parts of your body— one part controls speech.

cannot use his mouth in the same way others do, for instance, he may be unable to make certain sounds or say certain words. Others with speech impairment may have problems with breathing that cause them trouble when speaking. Since speaking involves so many body parts working correctly, a problem with one part can be a problem for the whole process.

Speech and Language Impairment: What's the Difference?

Though they are closely linked, speech and language impairments are not the same thing. Kids with speech impairments can have difficulties making the sounds needed for speaking. They may not be able to make sounds quickly enough to speak clearly and correctly, or they may have problems with the sound of their voice. Some kids may have more than one of these issues with speech. Most people with speech impairments understand how to use language correctly, but they have trouble actually speaking.

Examples of speech impairment:
- using one sound in place of another.
- speaking with a lisp—replacing the *s* and *z* sounds with a *th* sound.

- stuttering or stammering— breaks in the flow of speech, often due to repeating some sounds without meaning to.
- speaking too quickly or too slowly.
- changing some sounds so that they're hard to understand.
- volume or pitch problems.
- not being able to make some sounds.

Language impairments, on the other hand, get in the way of a person understanding or using language, even though she can correctly make the sounds needed for speech. A student with a language impairment may not be able to understand certain rules of language, for instance.

Kids with language impairments may:

- be easily *distracted* or unable to follow directions.
- have difficulties understanding the meaning of conversation, questions, or directions.

> *If you feel **distracted**, you are having a hard time paying attention or focusing.*

- learn language later than most children their age.
- use one word when wanting to use another, or use words incorrectly.
- have trouble using correct grammar.

What Causes Speech or Language Impairment?

Both speech and language impairments have many possible causes.

Speech impairments may be caused by many different types of disorders, diseases, or injuries. They may also be caused by a birth defect, a physical or mental problem that is there at birth.

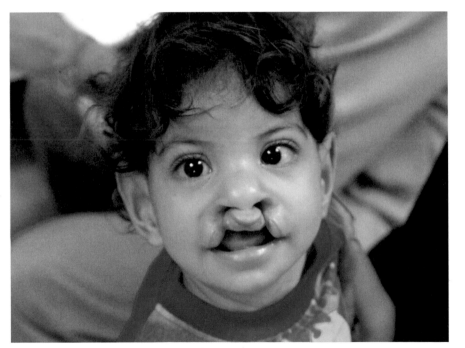

Though a cleft palate or lip can be fixed with surgery, it may still cause a speech impairment.

There are two types of speech impairment:

- expressive: If a child has difficulties making certain sounds, giving him trouble when speaking, then he has an *expressive* difficulty. An expressive problem is a problem with making the sounds of speech.
- receptive: If a child's speech impairment is because he has trouble hearing or understanding language that is spoken to him, he has a *receptive* issue. Receptive problems have to do with the ability to understand speech.

Speech impairments can be caused by:

- head injury
- loss of hearing before learning to speak

Expressive has to do with expressing yourself—putting your ideas into words.

Receptive has to do with receiving ideas—understanding what other people say to you.

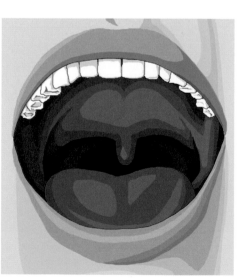

Your teeth, lips, tongue, and the roof of your mouth all play roles in speech.

- teeth being out of place
- cleft palate (A cleft palate means there is a space or hole in the roof of the mouth that can make clear speech difficult. A cleft palate is a type of birth defect and can be fixed through surgery.)
- cleft lip (A cleft lip is an upper lip that is split in the middle. It is another type of birth defect and can also be fixed through surgery.)

Language impairments can also be the result of many different problems. Oftentimes, disorders that damage the brain will get in the way of a child learning how to speak and understand language.

Language impairments can be caused by:
- head injury
- hearing loss before learning language
- *intellectual disability*
- *autism*

An *intellectual disability* means that a person will not learn as fast as other people.

Autism is a lifelong brain disorder that gets in the way of a person relating with others. People with autism may have below average, average, or above average intelligence, but regardless of their intelligence, they will have problems communicating and connecting emotionally with others.

- *schizophrenia*
- *abnormal* brain development
- *genetic* disorders

Diagnosing Speech Impairment

Diagnosing speech and language impairments early in a child's life can be very important so he can get the type of treatment he needs to succeed as he grows up. The earlier the diagnosis is made, the earlier a child can get special help in school and begin to work on his impairment.

Speech *pathologists* are experts who specialize in speech and language impairments. Only trained speech pathologists can diagnose and treat speech or language

Schizophrenia is a psychological disorder that causes a person to be unable to see reality. A person with schizophrenia may also not be able to communicate with others.

Something that is *abnormal* is not normal, usual, or healthy.

Genetic has to do with the traits that are passed down to a child by his parents.

Diagnosing is the process of figuring out what illness or disorder someone has.

Pathologists are doctors who are experts in certain diseases or disorders. Pathologists often specialize in specific illnesses or conditions.

impairments. They understand the signs of speech and language impairment, and can help children and adults with impairments get the treatment they need. Speech pathologists, sometimes called speech-language pathologists, work in schools, hospitals, and doctors' offices. Pathologists can also talk with family and teachers, making sure children are getting assistance both at home and in school.

When diagnosing speech and language impairments, a speech pathologist will speak with the child, closely listening to the way he speaks. The pathologist listens to

A speech pathologist works with a child to understand what his impairment is, and what help he needs.

the child's ability to make sounds correctly and easily. She makes sure the child is able to speak quickly enough for conversation and that the flow of speech is not broken by stuttering or by not being able to make certain sounds. Pathologists check that there are no issues in voice quality, pitch, or volume. Last, a pathologist will make sure the child does not have any problems in understanding and using language correctly.

Fluidly describes something that flows easily.

If a child cannot make the sounds of speech correctly or speak *fluidly*, she may be diagnosed with speech impair-

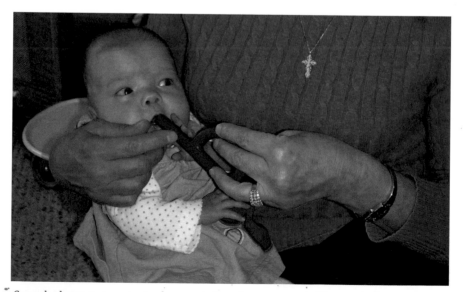

Speech therapy can start when an infant is very young. This pathologist is working with this little girl to help strengthen the muscles of her lips and face.

ment. A pathologist may diagnose a child with language impairment if she has difficulties understanding the rules of language, using words correctly, or has below-average language skills for her age.

Treating Speech Impairment

Each person's impairment is different, and treatment must fit the needs of the individual.

One of the most common types of treatment for speech or language impairment is called speech *therapy*. Speech therapy involves many different ways of teaching proper speech and communication to those with speech or language impairments. Therapy can be given by a speech therapist or a speech pathologist.

The therapist will often speak with a child's family and teachers so they can help the child remember to speak correctly at home and in the classroom. Speech therapists may recommend that kids with serious communication impairments be placed in special classrooms more focused on learning correct speech and language. Mostly,

Therapy is the treatment of physical and mental illnesses. Speech therapy involves teaching communication skills as a way of treating speech and language impairment.

however, children attend speech therapy a few times a week during school.

In addition to speech therapy, many kids with speech or language impairments use other tools to help them learn how to speak correctly and better understand language.

Here are a few examples:

- mirrors: Using a mirror, kids can compare the way their mouth, tongue, and lips move when making certain sounds with their therapist's.
- Califone machines: Califone machines record the voice of a patient onto a card. The card can be read by the Califone machine and play back the recording of the

Mirrors are often part of speech therapy—they allow the child to see how her mouth and tongue move during speech.

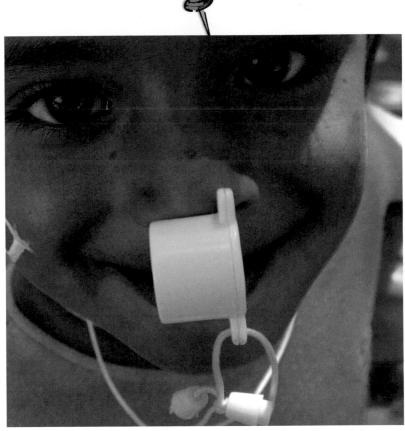

Whistles can also be used as part of speech therapy. The act of blowing a whistle helps strengthen a child's mouth and lips.

student's voice, helping her understand what she sounds like.

- whistles: Whistles can be used to help strengthen a patient's mouth and lips.

Speech Impairment and School

Communication is at the heart of learning in school. If you can't understand what your teacher is saying, it will be hard for you to learn—and if she can't understand what you are saying, it will be hard for her to help you learn. As kids grow older, they are expected to learn more and more complicated ideas and express themselves clearly. In order to keep up with their friends and classmates, children with speech impairments must work hard to overcome the challenges they face.

Not all kids with speech and language impairments need *special education*, but some do. A law known as the Individuals with Disabilities Education Act, or IDEA, describes how schools decide which kids need special education. In order to *qualify* for IDEA, the child's condition must get in the way of him learning or taking part in school activities.

Special education teaches kids who have trouble learning because of some disability.

To qualify means to fit the definition of something or to meet the requirements.

A category is a group or a certain kind of thing.

The IDEA law lists thirteen different kinds of disabilities that may mean a child will need special education. Speech and language problems fall under a *category* in IDEA called "communication disorders."

A child with a speech or language impairment may need special education to help her succeed in school.

In order for a child to receive special education, the law requires that:

- the child has problems performing well at school activities.

Get to know a child with a speech or language impairment and you will find she is not that different from you!

- the child's parent, teacher, or other school staff person must ask that the child be examined for a disability.
- the child is *evaluated* to decide if she does indeed have a disability and to figure out what kind of special education she needs.
- a group of people, including the kid's parents, teachers, and a school psychologist, meets to decide on a plan for helping him. This plan is called an Individualized

> When something is *evaluated*, it is examined to see in which category it belongs.

Education Program (IEP). The IEP spells out exactly what the child needs in order to succeed at school, and who will be involved in making sure he gets the help he needs. A speech therapist would be an important part of this plan for all students with speech or language disorders.

Speech Impairment and Feelings

Talking is a big part of everything you do, whether it's learning in a classroom, playing on the playground, or eating dinner with your family. Being able to share your thoughts and feelings with others is important to how you feel about yourself. So imagine if you couldn't make people understand you! You'd probably feel frustrated . . . embarrassed . . . and lonely.

You can help kids with speech and language impairments. Here are a few ways:

- Kids with speech impairments may be shyer than others. They may not speak as often as kids without speech impairments. When they do speak, they may feel embarrassed. Put yourself in their place and imagine how you would feel. Treat them with the same respect you'd want shown to you.
- Be patient. Kids with speech or language impairments may need more time to answer questions, express an idea, or communicate a thought.
- Be kind. Embarrassment often makes speech problems worse. If you let a person know you like him, he'll be more able to relax and communicate more clearly.

Did You Know?

Between 1 in 10 and 1 in 20 children have some issues with speech or language.

Further Reading

Bryant, J. E. *Taking Speech Disorders to School*. Plainview, N.Y.: JayJo Books, 2004.

Dougherty, D. P. *Teach Me How to Say It Right: Helping Your Child With Articulation Problems*. Oakland, Calif.: New Harbinger Publications, 2005.

Feit, D. *The Parent's Guide to Speech and Language Problems*. New York: McGraw-Hill, 2007.

Kent, S. *Let's Talk About Stuttering*. New York: Rosen Publishing, 2000.

MacDonald, J. and P. Stoika. *Play to Talk: A Practical Guide to Help Your Late-Talking Child Join the Conversation*. Madison, Wis.: Kiddo Publishing, 2007.

Martin, K. L. *Does My Child Have A Speech Problem?* Chicago, Ill.: Chicago Review Press, 1997.

Sowell, T. *The Einstein Syndrome: Bright Children Who Talk Late*. New York: Basic Books, 2001.

St. Louis, K. O., ed. *Living with Stuttering: Stories, Basics, Resources, and Hope*. Morgantown, W.V.: Populore Publishing Company, 2001.

Wojcicki, R. M. *Speech Class Rules: An Introduction to Speech Therapy for Children*. Lutherville, Ma.: The Speech Place Publishing, 2007.

Find Out More On the Internet

Canadian Association of Speech-Language Pathologists
and Audiologists
www.caslpa.ca

Childhood Apraxia of Speech Association
www.apraxia-kids.org

Children's Speech Care Center
www.childspeech.net

ISA (International Stuttering Association)
www.stutterisa.org

National Dissemination Center for Children with Disabilities
(NICHCY)
www.nichcy.com

Stuttering Foundation of America
www.stutteringhelp.org

Disclaimer

The websites listed on this page were active at the time of publication. The publisher is not responsible for websites that have changed their address or discontinued operation since the date of publication. The publisher will review and update the websites upon each reprint.

Index

About the Authors

Sheila Stewart has written several dozen books for young people, both fiction and nonfiction, although she especially enjoys writing fiction. She has a master's degree in English and now works as a writer and editor. She lives with her two children in a house overflowing with books, in the Southern Tier of New York State.

Camden Flath is a writer living and working in Binghamton, New York. He has a degree in English and has written several books for young people. He is interested in current political, social, and economic issues and applies those interests to his writing.

About the Consultant

Dr. Carolyn Bridgemohan is board certified in developmental behavioral pediatrics and practices at the Developmental Medicine Center at Children's Hospital Boston. She is the director of the Autism Care Program and an assistant professor at Harvard Medical School. Her specialty areas are autism and other pervasive developmental disorders, developmental and learning problems, and developmental and behavioral pediatrics.